A JOURNEY THROUGH BLACK SOUTHERN CHRISTIANITY

Dasan Ahanu

WILLOW BOOKS
Detroit, Michigan

A Month of Sundays

Cover art: Gemynii
Author photo: Stan Chambers, Jr.

ISBN 9781734827361

Willow Books, a Division of Aquarius Press
www.WillowLit.net

Printed in the United States of America

Contents

Preface

I was sitting in my Nanny's church one Sunday when the pastor said something that dramatically changed my thoughts about church. He said the church was the body of believers, not the building. Mathew 18:20 says, "For where two or three gather in my name, there am I with them." This scripture was monumental for me. It was the moment that I learned that the people are what matters. When people come together in faith, that's church. When people come together in purpose and will, it is church. When people come together to lift their voices and spirits in making a joyful noise, it is church. God is with us. Favor is with us. Grace is with us.

This concept of church is something that I would hear from poets and other artists. These creatives, who grew up being taken to church by our mothers and big mamas, saw the church in our gatherings. We saw open mics, showcases, exhibitions, and jam sessions as spiritual moments where the best of us came out, where we bared our souls, where we were able to be vulnerable, hopeful, resilient, and faithful. Spaces so powerful we could only leave them feeling as if we had just been in the presence of glory—the joy in our hearts and smiles accompanied by a hallelujah and amen.

This place we gather is our dirt church, a remnant of the clearings where Black folks gathered to fellowship and lament, where Black folks fed each other and their spirits. These Hush Harbors were where enslaved people mixed what they were given with what they knew as a way of figuring out how to make it through what they were dealing with. I think about the necessity of that focus when artists gather. Wherever we gather, God is with us. Favor is with us. Grace is with us. Radical Voice is present there.

In *Everything Worth Fighting For: An Exploration of Being Black in America*, I defined Radical Voice.

Radical Voice is a distinctive manner of expression aimed at the root or origin of an issue; favoring drastic political, economic, or social change; and conveying revolutionary and redemptive principles inherent in radical social movements.

This definition came from the Radical Voice and Artistic Expression (RVAE) project I started in 2014. My goal with the project was to actively connect art and artists to an integrated strategy for radical transformation. In conjunction with that work, I began to work on a book of poetry that reflected the principles of that project. I envisioned it as the first in a three-part series. That first book was *Everything Worth Fighting For: An Exploration of Being Black in America.*

The second book was *Shackled Freedom: Black Living in the Modern American South.* That collection is my love letter to the South in which I live. It is a recognition of the beauty, brilliance, and strength in the South that I love. In that book, I talk about my goal to help artists continue thinking about how their work can foster transformation. The Black South is my proof of concept. The Black South is my training ground. It is also my breakthrough model.

In these two books, I convey how artistic movements are social movements and that art communities/scenes share many characteristics of social movements. There are even similarities in their rhetoric. Both are where you can see redemptive and revolutionary/transformative impact. Because of these similarities, I developed a project that campaigned for integrated efforts to include art and artists in movements focused on change. For me, that starts in the South. A South where Black folks understand struggle and fight—a South where Black art is bountiful and magical. Black art represents all we have faced, dealt with, and overcome. There is a model for resistance in this country, and it has its foundation in the Black South. The Black South is where Radical Voice is so resounding.

The Hush Harbors led to Praise Houses. These Praise Houses led to the Black church. Our dirt church can lead to theatres and museums. The deepening of our craft can then lead us to concert halls and academic institutions. We can find ourselves on TV and Radio, even in films. Each opportunity is a chance to have a church moment with the people. To center the stories of our lives, the wishes of our hearts, the falter in our spirits, and the burdens on our shoulders. We welcome everyone to fellowship with us. We call them into a worship moment that is intended for the whole of us. We claim our victory and affirm our commitment. In our art we mix what we are given with what we know as a way of figuring out how to make it through what we are all dealing with.

This series' third installment is focused on Black Southern Christianity. To do so feels so very important to me. I was taught that church is where believers are gathered. I found that to be true in so many ways. I not only found church where I gathered with artists. I found church when I gathered with activists to fight for social justice. I found church planning demonstrations, trainings, and actions intended to provide marginalized and oppressed folks with support, encouragement, and options. I saw glory in each space. I saw radical voices making a joyful noise.

I also understood that many sought these spaces where folks were gathered because they felt that the buildings intended for church were no longer holding to intent and mission. The Black church has long been a cornerstone of African American communities, serving as a spiritual center and a powerful catalyst for social change. It had to be both. Our faith was part of how we equipped ourselves for our ongoing struggle for our worth, rights, and self-determination. The Black church was pivotal in advancing social justice movements for many years. The church was a headquarters, a place to strategize and coordinate actions and efforts. The church was a place to debrief. The church was a place to celebrate and affirm, all to re-energize folks to go out and fight again.

From the clearing to the sanctuary, religious leaders within the Black church would use their pulpit as a space to address issues of slavery, inequality, brutality, disenfranchisement, and the quest for freedom. We saw the Black church become a hub for organizing protests, marches, and acts of civil disobedience. It provided a moral framework for challenging discriminatory laws and practices, emphasizing the principles of justice, equality, and love for one's neighbor.

Thing is… somewhere along the lines, something changed.

In RVAE, we say that Radical Voice is a multi-genre artistic agitation intended to exert influence and inspire change. A business principle outlined by Albert O. Hirschman in Exit, Voice, and Loyalty that identifies "exit" and "voice" as strategies for expressing dissatisfaction with an entity inspires this framework. "Exit" is quitting use or association or switching to a competitor. "Voice" is to agitate and exert influence for change "from within."

This last installment in this poetry series is me exerting influence for change from within. This book is me using my Voice to agitate, challenge, and call to question. This book is me trying to help us all recognize that somewhere along the lines, something changed. It is the book of a believer who has had a chance to have church with others who believe too in spaces that the pious would never call holy. It is the work of a believer who found other believers wondering why they didn't feel welcome in the buildings designated as sanctuaries. It is the cry of a believer who wonders why some feel our liberation comes with a caveat of respectability.

I am inviting you into this here dirt church. A place where I am going to mix what I have been given with what I have seen, heard, and experienced to call us to think about how we are going to make it through what we are dealing with.

We can't have social change without art and artists. I am not talking about art as an accent and artists as a celebratory partner. I am not talking about artists as a distant observer and their art as historical marker. I mean art and artists as an integrated part of a strategy for liberation.

We cannot have liberation without faith. Whatever faith is to you and wherever it comes from, it is necessary. For me, that faith is what I learned from my grandmothers. It is what they had in that clearing. It is what my grandmothers found in that churchhouse. It is a faith I carry with me into the most beautiful and rebellious spaces. It is a faith that assures me we will win. A faith modeled by the two most powerful forces of nature I have ever known.

We cannot afford not to have all the conversations needed to ensure we fight for a tomorrow we can all celebrate. That means talking about the tools we need to win. That means talking about the cadre we need to win. That means talking about the resilient faith we need to win. This book is me attempting to have one of those conversations.

By turning the pages of this book, you are joining the conversation. I hope you are ready.

Welcome.

Foreword

My mama used to hum songs to Jesus while frying chicken. It is the first thought that came to mind upon reading *Month of Sundays*, Dasan Ahanu's newest masterpiece. It aroused countless memories of the Black women who saved my soul when the devil and the enemies of my freedom came knocking at the door. Those Black women rescued me from thoughts placed in my head after I did my own share of ruinous living.

It is good to know I am not the only Black man protected by the prayers of Black women dedicated to teaching lessons about true freedom. These poems capture the testimonies behind what church folks call a covering. My mama keeps covering me in the same way my grandmas, great-grandmas and the many clouds of Black women witnesses prayed for the Black men in my family lineage.

Ahanu captures something deep in my soul. Mine is a thought about grace beyond anything deserved by me and other men who take love for granted. After all the bad mouthing about what Black women fail to do - combined with a myriad of lies and abuse – Black women have an ability to love the unlovable part of Black men.

It is humbling to admit not deserving the love of Black women. There's magic in their love empowered by an authentic understanding of the power of the Holy Ghost. There's redemption in the will of a Black women to embrace Black men. They recognize the image of God in us when we waddle in the misery of decay caused by our own decisions.

It is why I am convinced the spirit of the resurrected Christ comes in the form of a Black woman. Black women understand a life of virulent rejection. Black women fully comprehend the cruelty of crucifixion and the pain of being falsely accused. How many Black women have cried, "Father, forgive him cause he don't know what he doing?" How many Black women have wept alone after her man left her without the support she needs?

I am not surprised when Ahanu writes, "At my grandma's house every meal was a holy communion. A roadmap to an alter and a restoration of the promise I made God." Black men baptized in the love and care of faithful Black women understand a faith more powerful than the words recited from the Good Book.

I have been listening to Ahanu's poems for more than twenty years. I dubbed him the minster of poetry at Compassion Ministries of Durham, a church I founded after getting kicked out of another church for being too liberal for Southern Black Christians. Ahanu was part of a group of young, progressive believers in search of a deeper relationship with Jesus. The faith of their grandparents offered enough to bring them through many dangers' toils and snares, but they needed more after their souls became weary due to thoughts not answered in the Bible.

After being kicked out of the church for teaching liberation, Ahanu offered poems that stirred my soul with the liberating power of God's Good News. Each poem healed the part of me missing after the holy men and women of that Baptist church pronounced me unworthy of continued service as a minister of God's grace and mercy.

When Ahanu writes:

"My prayers are for the
Restoration of my faith and
discernment. While I wonder
If the failure was in what
those saints refuse to see
In you or what they refuse
to see in me."

A part of me feels exposed. Another poem designed for a growing body of believers. We are the body of believers abandoned by Christians who remain submissive to the teachings of old-time religion. We are the believers who feel the love and compassion of

Jesus. Is the failure "in what those saints refuse to see in you." You - Jesus with a heart to love beyond gender identity or other human created constructs. Is the failure in "what they refuse to see in me" – a man committed to loving and caring for every person created in the image of God.

Month of Sundays is more than an anthology of poems about religion. Ahanu provides theological discourse for an emerging Black faith community. These poems evoke the collective cries of Black spiritual refugees. These are the moans of Black men and women aching to reconcile the faith of their Black mothers and grandmothers with a newfound determination for authentic liberation.

When Ahanu writes:

"Talented tenth
A long day's work
Black exceptionalism
Southern grown dialect
Nonviolent resistance
Black Power
Disco chic
Hip Hop rebellion
Round the way
Upwardly mobile
HBCU
PWI
Jay Z
Nas"

I feel the weight of division in the Black community. I hear Jesus spitting poetry regarding the haves and have nots. I hear parables related to false security – the first shall be last, and the last shall be first. I feel the tension within the Bible aimed at undoing notions of fake security and power grabs rooted in the assumptions of white supremacy.

I read poems digging deeper into a theology of liberation for all Black people. These messages are more transforming than pull up your pants and speak like you have good sense. This is a theology of God's grace transcendent of the claims of talented tenth. There is rich, Good News, in the rapology of Jay Z and Naz. God speaks within the witness of Black Power, Hip Hop and is present on both HBCU and PWI campuses.

God is much bigger than all our assumptions.

Ahanu is seeking clarity and perspective – a merging of the faith of his matriarch and his experience as a disciple of Hip Hop culture. This is the grappling of a new perspective to faith. It is part of an emerging body of theological work among children of Hip Hop culture.

Faith seeking understanding is the classical definition of theology. Faith in God prompts a questioning search for deeper understanding.

When my mama hummed to Jesus while frying chicken, her faith was seeking understanding. Hums are questions regarding how much longer and why bad things happen to good people.

Ahanu has a list of questions. He calls them *Month of Sundays*. I call it good theology.

Sounds like God's good news.

Can I get a witness?

-       **Carl W. Kenney II**

Carl W. Kenney II is an award-winning columnist and novelist. He is committed to engaging readers into a meaningful discussion related to matters that impact faith and society. He grapples with pondering the impact faith has on public space while seeking to understand how public space both hinders and enhances the walk of faith.

Introduction

Whatever faith helped my people survive this long in a country that has never loved us is a believing I can't imagine disrupting or dismissing right now. Not when that faith has been the reason why folks show up to fight. Not when it's why we're able to keep showing up to do work. When it has been both salve and fuel. Whatever it is, folks have earned the right to have it. You got no business bothering it.

I learned about faith from both of my grandmothers. I ain't never seen nothing like how they held families together, made a way, and made it through. I only know miracles are possible because I saw them celebrate them. I know prayer works because of how much time they spent on their knees, hand clasped, in conversation with God about their babies. I know that the lessons they taught us are still with us, even though those two matriarchs have gone on home. I never saw apathy. I never saw complacency. I saw two Black women who held onto a strong relationship with their God and a pistol. I saw a powerful conviction that persevered again and again. So, what they were, I am. You can't shake me from it.

So many of us have our models. Models that have nothing to do with the prevailing presence of systems or institutions of belief. They have to do with people's real lived experiences with angels and prophets more tangible than biblical. The very present and real embodiments of holy and blessed that exist. The moments that are understood more by spirit than mind. The testimonies that are both a joyful noise and a good word.

I took time to study and research. After doing so I came back to the faith I grew up knowing. I chose where I wanted to sit and what I would use as my compass. I chose tangible examples of faith in practice. Because ideology and theory have been tools of manipulation for centuries. My reference points are those matriarchs, those folks... those communities . . . the fighters.

If you have something else to offer that can glue someone whole through all that they have to deal with, offer it. If not, leave what they have to use alone. It doesn't matter how you feel about what folks' faith is, respect it. That's all. You don't have to agree. Just respect it. It's tied to more than a doctrine or a spiritual oligarchy.

Top-down you can always find problems (corruption, indulgence, power hungriness, benevolent patriarchy, and more). Bottom-up what you find is the beautiful resilience and determination and recontextualization we have always had. We make things work for us and create spaces we feel safe in. Our presence in and beyond a thing is a duality we have mastered since we were brought here. It's part of our magic. We know what it means to be in it. Gone do what we need to do to survive it. Know what it looks like to be beyond it. Gone be driven by an understanding that we are more than any circumstance. We are shapeshifters and alchemists. We will make it be what it needs to be. I've seen it firsthand.

These poems are a reminder of all the ways this faith can show up. A reminder that our relationship with God is beyond a day of the week. With us, there is a month of Sundays.

—Dasan Ahanu

Heaven Was a Place Called Home

John 1:1—In the beginning was the Word, and the Word was with God, and the Word was God

In the beginning
was my momma,
and my momma
was with God,
my momma was God
My momma was the light
and the way
Single parent
So, in our house,
all things came from God
Without her
I would not have made it
This son of optimism
that said work with my father
until you realize
he likes the making of a child
but wasn't prepared
for the rest
We call the day he said goodbye
the sabbath
Consider it holy

I am my momma's child
Given favor for believing in her
Seen her make miracles
out of nothing
Seen her raise the dead
of my self-worth
when the world misunderstood
my awkward
Gave me this light

Told me to shine
Gave me a good word
Told me to share
So here it is
Not born of blood,
or flesh, but of faith
My momma's faith in me
I serve a benevolent God
Gave me everything she could
Made me everything I am

It is her grace and mercy
that covers me
It is her likeness I carry
It is her judgement I fear
The revelations of my mistakes
coming back to haunt me
It is redemption I find
when I call on her
to see the man I have become
and she says that it is good

Isn't it good
To know
the glory of God
To say you saw it
firsthand

Insatiable Hunger

Psalm 34:8—Taste and see that the LORD is good; blessed is the one who takes refuge in him.

At my grandma's house
every meal was a holy communion
A roadmap to an altar
and a restoration
of the promise I made God
before being dipped in water

I lost that last mapmaker I knew
in the midst of a May hot streak
Tears streaming from my cheek
My lungs an overactive window unit
trying to cool my sweltering pain

Now I don't know where else to go
Don't know no place fit
to show me where my faith lies
other than her stove and rickety table
That kitchen was a church
where salvation was cooked all day
and left waiting with plate, knife, and fork

The only thing I can think to do
is try to recipe a remembrance
The only penance I can offer
is time spent with pots and pans
Hoping I can fill the house
with a scriptured seasoning
and be assured that I am still deserved
of a blessing

Road to Sobriety

James 1:3—because you know that the testing of your faith develops perseverance

I sometimes believe
that my daddy was drinking
until our prayers were answered

I don't know whether to blame God
or say Amen

A Tale of Two Mothers

1 Kings 3:27—Then the king said, "Do not kill him, but give the baby to the woman who wants him to live, for she is his mother!"

Lady Liberty and
Mother Africa asked
for a day in court.

Mother Africa wanted
her stolen children back.

Lady Liberty said they were hers.

We are still waiting for Solomon
to arrive.

Because the number of dead black babies
left in tumultuous seas was harrowing.

The number of black babies
being cut down in city streets
is deafening.

A Moment with God

Acts 18:11—So Paul stayed for a year and a half, teaching them the word of God.

My stepfather
played bass guitar
in a gospel group
Traveled making a
joyful noise
Plucking strings
Singing

He was a mechanic
by trade
Fixed cars
Serviced them until
they were running
again

My stepfather
put a smile on
my momma's face
Gave me a reason
to think I had a
role model

It hurt when they
got divorced
I cried
Felt left behind
Another father running
again

I wish I had learned
to play the guitar

I wished I had learned
to fix a car
But what I did learn is
what it's like to know a
version of God
that wasn't just
an ominous presence

What I had
was a chance to know
a truth that was present
that was more than
a non child supported
immaculate conception

Art Imitating Faith

Heb 12:2—Let us fix our eyes on Jesus, the author and perfecter of our faith, who for the joy set before him endured the cross, scorning its shame, and sat down at the right hand of the throne of God

I asked God for a miracle.
Was given a poem.
Told to be Christlike
in my artistry.

I was treated exactly
the same.

So, for the sake of my sanity
I disappear 3 days at a time.

I tell them to prepare for the day
I leave.
Instead,
they prefer to prepare for the day
I return.

Heartache on Sundays

1 Cor 10:13—No temptation has seized you except what is common
to man. And God is faithful; he will not let you be tempted beyond
what you can bear. But when you are tempted, he will also provide a
way out so that you can stand up under it.

Church folks thought us the same,
you and I. But alas,
I am the prayers of a
God fearing woman.
You are the last snide remark
the Devil made
before leaving heaven.
The belief in anything made
of us was a falsehood
I hope to be forgiven for.
My prayers are for the
restoration of my faith and
discernment. While I wonder
if the failure was in what
those saints refused to see
in you or what they refuse
to see in me.

Learning from Goldwater

Matthew 16:26—What good will it be for a man if he gains the whole world, yet forfeits his soul? Or what can a man give in exchange for his soul?

My uncle came home
from desert storm
searching for peace
Searching for a way
to calm the chaos
and escape the nightmares
He found a resonate prophecy
on a street corner
Brought home the books
and tapes
Spoke of righteousness
and wickedness
I wondered if he saw the irony

For a moment
he was happy
My family stayed worried
They were good Christians
Church going folks
who had never considered conspiracies,
only the power of faith
Knew how to call on his name
Not how to call
to question

Unfortunately,
the knowledge
wasn't enough
Soon the smile
started to fade

Then the rest
of him followed
Before long he was a shell
of the joy that enlisted
His tour of duty
had robbed him
of more than
any level of consciousness
could replace
His soul lost

From my uncle
I learned that
there are no facts
that can hold you whole
No learning that can
restore the sunshine
once your dawn
has been taken away,
replaced with midnight
and a thank you

In that moment
I learned about the world
my uncle had been
consumed by
Learned the value of faith
Learned to never
give mine away to anyone
Learned to seek faith
but know my God,
know who I am, and
know that my uncle
gave what was left of him
so that I can live
eyes open

Like Water from the Rock

Numbers 20:10-11-10— Then he and Aaron summoned the people to come and gather at the rock. "Listen, you rebels!' he shouted. "Must we bring you water from this rock?" 11 Then Moses raised his hand and struck the rock twice with the staff, and water gushed out. So all the people and their livestock drank their fill.

My second stepfather was a proud man
who loved to show off the fruits
of THEIR marriage to anyone
willing to pay attention
to all HE had achieved

I haven't seen him much
since the divorce

Prayer 7779311

1 Corinthians 13:13—So now faith, hope, and love abide, these three;
but the greatest of these is love.

You are an oasis in a desert
i've been crawling across for too long,
parched for your kiss and
dying for the hope of your embrace.

I feel you in the soles of my shoes.
Each step is a vagabond's journey
towards the home I dream you
have been redecorating for me.

I found a bumble bee with a prayer
pollinating the location of our next picnic.
A woodpecker with its bill dipped in ink
inscribing directions to you in oak.

I will follow the setting sun to your doorstep.
Your kiss reminding me why we hate summer.

Naked Offering

Rom 12:1—Therefore, I urge you, brothers, in view of God's mercy, to offer your bodies as living sacrifices, holy and pleasing to God—this is your spiritual act of worship.

I have made my body
sacrificial lamb
for more late-night rituals
than I care to admit
Given myself as offering
because I believed the cries
to our father
whose art
becomes limbs water painted
onto bedsheets amidst sweat
and a damning insatiability
was a joyful noise

The tongues I speak are prophetic
They tell of a coming
that will quickly after
fall victim to betrayal
Here latex has a Judas complex
Together
we've martyred more possible blossoms
than I can pray forgiveness for
When they die for this sin
I consider them devout
Call them my flock
that I have taught to lay down
their lives for a higher purpose

This is what you do for mercy,
for favor
This is what you do to calm a storm

or temper locusts
When despair is the aftermath
of your last lover's exodus
When she marked your penis
as safe,
but left your heart to be ravaged
So now you split legs
trying to escape the pain
Claiming victory when the orgasm
floods the memories away
You consider yourself free

For a moment

Until your emotions go awry
Placing faith in strokes, moans,
and golden package saviors

I have been forty-year fucking
my way to a promised land
I don't even know if I would
recognize anymore

How long can you attempt
to beat down the walls of Jericho
before you just give up hope

I don't even know if I understand
how to give praise without this
slaughter
This is what we do here
Loneliness is a vengeance
I want no part of
So, I offer myself
as a plattered passion
Laid out

With the hope
that it will be deemed good,
worthy,
enough

Enough

ENOUGH

Armed Strong

II Corinthians 12:9-10 - 9—But he said to me, my grace is sufficient for you, for my power is made perfect in weakness." Therefore I will boast all the more gladly about my weaknesses, so that Christ's power may rest on me. 10 That is why, for Christ's sake, I delight in weaknesses, in insults, in hardships, in persecutions, in difficulties. For when I am weak, then I am strong."

I have built a fort
of my missteps
in the middle of my living room

I hide there
when I need to be reminded
of a soldier's discipline
to the land it protects

I raise an eye at half mast
when someone sends
my love back
in a casket

Trumpet a cry
Rifle tears in a salute
to the service
my hapless romanticism
considers a tour of duty

The next sunrise I thank God,
then begin morning maneuvers
Prepare my optimism
for battle
A deployment into foreign lands
with the hope of establishing
a happy ending

Peace be Still

Romans 8:18—"I consider that our present sufferings are not worth comparing with the glory that will be revealed in us."

It was a little after fo'
when gossip found Henry
enjoying a calm Thursday eve
on his front porch.

Seems there was someone
across town with a grudge
and a lot of shit to say 'bout Henry
who was talking to anybody
who would listen.

Henry tipped the mason jar
towards his mouth,
took a long swig, and
then poured some stump
onto the grass.

Libation he said,
for the ancestors who gave
him the wisdom to ignore
simple minded foolishness.

If it was that damn important, he said,
those words would've been
spoken on this porch.

And instead of liquor,
what would've hit
that grass woulda been
somebody's ass after he knocked
them the hell out.

A Pastor Named Earl

John 16:33—"I have told you these things, so that in me you may have peace. In this world you will have trouble. But take heart! I have overcome the world."

They ain't never seen nothing
like Earl Ray
Ain't never heard an applause
like the earth under each step
Ain't never witnessed
the sky bend to will
until you hear the wind
whistle his arrival
Sounded like a warrior's reverie
Ain't too many decorated
like Earl Ray

They say that nigga
held dawn between his lips
Gave it to any woman
trying to see her way free of the dark
Say you knew last night was over
when you saw Earl smile
He liked to say he lost
his virginity to Mother Nature
Licked the sun from between her legs
and learned his stroke
from a summer breeze
Any of his yesterdays
will tell you that won't all
he left with
Say his spirit was a natural disaster
Heart was midnight

Earl laid bricks 10 hours a day

He knew hard work
But the made bed and
warm meal came easy
It was reward for knowing
another morning was coming,
that the sun would rise again
Paid by anyone willing
to accept Earl's fancy
as adequate return
Willing to accept that
any man that lost his virginity
in the midst of coming seasons
couldn't be anything
other than fair weather

Earl had a storm of a temper
One Saturday night at the bar
turned all thunder and lightning
That was the night jealousy came looking
Seems the last bed laid and
breakfast made used to belong
to someone who's broken heart
saw redemption as blood and bruises
He should've known Earl's hands
were dark clouds
dense and powerful
Ended up on the wrong side
of a tempest
It was all flood and hail
Earl damn near beat that man
a morning after rainbow

Three years outta county
Earl was a changed man
Found his calm in the midst
of an old bible

Found his home in a church
They ain't never seen nobody
preach like Earl Ray
Ain't never heard an applause
like the affirmation for his good word
Ain't never witnessed
the will of God take over
until you hear the cries of joy
and feel the building shake an amen
Sounded like glory
came from up on high
and overtook the congregation
cuz Earl Ray said so

They say that nigga
memorized righteousness in jail
Gave it to any lost soul
trying to see their way free of the dark
Say you knew last night was over
when you heard Earl quote scripture
He liked to say he lost
the devil inside and found salvation
Found grace between an Angel's wings
and learned that he had never
been foresaken
Any of his yesterdays
would be forgiven
if he called on the Lord
He left that jailhouse restored
Said his spirit was a natural disaster
But thank God he was shown
that a blue sky was possible

A baker's dozen later
they say Earl looking regal
His better way came with 5 bedrooms,

a Mercedes Benz, and a tailor
Say ain't nobody seen nothing
like Earl Ray
First Lady pretending ain't no more
A baby with a dawn's smile
that nobody speaks of
Earl still working storms
Sermons filled with fire and brimstone
and collection plate calls
for sinners to repent
That nigga done built the church
into a planetarium and
got half the town paying extra
for clear skies

A Savior is Born

1 Corinthians 16:13—Be on your guard; stand firm in the faith; be courageous; be strong.

In the house at the end
of the street
they call Mr. Jenkins
a jealous god.
Say he tells Hattie Mae
to put no other before him.
Say in his house,
to disobey him
leads to floods and earthquakes
Tells Hattie the plague of his wrath
is a lesson
Their children call it
Old Testament

When the baby boy was born
Social Services came
bearing an inquiry
Left with reports of a son happy
and a father who hadn't
been laying hands on his mother
Their wisdom in these situations
made it hard to believe
but Hattie swore it was true
At least the visit put Mr. Jenkins on notice
For that there was some joy,
but the scare was a temporary peace

Soon that boy learned
the burden of being
a god's son
When that blessed prodigy had finally

had enough
he decided his purpose
was to sacrifice himself
for his family
His mother was overcome with worry
about what the world would think
What they would do
He cared not
The only thing that mattered
was their salvation

He told everyone
of this god
His words red with anger
His heart filled with a passion to free
them from persecution
Everywhere he shared the word
they called it miracle
Didn't know how the family survived
Saw him as saving grace
Each statement scriptured
into reports, charges
Affirmed by the testimony
of those who witnessed
He held to his mission
until he made believers
of the authorities
and helped them understand
the work that needed
to be done

His gift was the greatest
he could give
He had come to understand
that his feelings of being forsaken
was the necessary spark

in his spirit to do
what no one else
was prepared to do
A martyred love
A promise to his family
that they would see
a better tomorrow
A covenant made
with his family
that they would live
the rest of their lives
free from their
father's sins

Art School Dropouts

1 Cor 10:13—No temptation has seized you except what is common to man. And God is faithful; he will not let you be tempted beyond what you can bear. But when you are tempted, he will also provide a way out so that you can stand up under it.

There are people who will try
to break you and call it love
Look at the shards of you
and claim themselves artist
Tell you they can
make you mosaic,
make you collage,
make you quilt,
make you stained glass,
make you beautiful
if you commit to their vision
of who you really should be
and ignore who they truly are

Divided

Genesis 13:8—Then Abram talked it over with Lot. "This arguing between our herdsmen has got to stop," he said. "After all, we are close relatives!"

Talented tenth
A long day's work
Black exceptionalism
Southern grown dialect
Nonviolent resistance
Black Power
Disco chic
Hip Hop rebellion
Round the way
Upwardly mobile
HBCU
PWI
Jay Z
Nas

Uncle Jimmy ain't came to a cookout
since Aunt Pat got remarried
to his high school rival
A petty and misguided boycott
he stayed committed to
even though he got caught cheating
with the counselor at their
daughter's school.

So, as we sit wondering if we are supposed to
call the new nigga Uncle
my cousin asks me if I saw the video
of ole dude in a Phillies hat
talking 'bout how somebody else
will never be 6'3"

Corinth County

Acts 18:10—For I am with you, and no one is going to attack and harm you, because I have many people in this city.

There is a privilege
to being connected
A reward attached
to the last name
your daddy gave you
Might be the only thing
he gave you of any value
Round these parts,
the features in your face,
the lean in your gait, and
the first three people you mention
when questioned
can be your saving grace

Great great great granddaddy
was the first Black
His son the first Black doctor
Your great uncle owned
the watering hole
most beloved by coal to caramel,
colored sinners and saints alike
Your grandmama taught school
for longer than the Walmart been here
Ain't too many that ain't called
her classroom a fond memory
You got a legacy round here
You got eyes on you round here

This is the ace in the hole
that allows your momma
to sleep well at night

They see your daddy in your eyes
but see a responsibility past
his ignorance
They rarely mention his name
Just ask if you Miss Mabel's boy
like yo momma was just a surrogate
Ask if you the same Jenkins
that's etched into the side
of the city auditorium
Ask if you know you ain't
supposed to be here
doing that
right now

You never ask why when you told
to go on home
Just know it be for a good reason
You never second guess
the dap given by stranger
The greeting seemingly diffusing
a land mine situation
you won't prepared for the blast of
Just thought you was
Won't refuse the courtesy,
the smiles,
the extra portions on your plate,
the free entry paid for
long before you was born

You was taught to be thankful
To recognize blessings
To appreciate the value
of guardian angels
and path laid

Instructions for Discipleship

Luke 11:10—For everyone who asks receives, and the one who seeks
finds, and to the one who knocks it will be opened

You don't show up
at a Black cookout
    unannounced
There better be somebody
waiting for you to arrive
Upon being met at the door
    or just outside your car
your first mission is to identify
the host of the party
Then there is a progression
of grateful to be distributed
Momma, Big Momma, Daddy,
and Granddaddy
    In that order

Remember,
you are entering sacred space
    Hallowed ground
The last refuge
from a world that believes
Black joy a blasphemy
Those smiles are not
manufactured for white gaze
    They are real
That laughter is deep and guttural
That music has SOUL and feeling
The food was made with love
Even the dishes dismissed to the far table
    A warning
Every offering is welcome
even if uneaten

God makes no mistakes
It was the devil that brought
that foolishness in here covered in foil
Don't find yourself exiled
The other side of the room
is a lonely purgatory

You are a guest on probation
The first 30 minutes after intros
is the most important
That is when you will be scrutinized
by cousins, aunties, uncles,
and family friends
The kids will taunt you
They like to toss toys to pit bulls
    round here
The significant others will
try to save you
They know this gauntlet
    Find them
Keep an eye on them
Any shake of the head
is a signal to abort
Take the advice
It is better to look fool
than ass

Here,
celebration is a rebellion
and a communion
On days like this
Big Mama's prayers
are animated for all to see
You must learn the characters,
know your role, and
not drop your lines

You are just providing voiceover
for the you they think they see
You have not put in enough time
to be real yet
   This is a choir
Get offered a solo
Take it
   Mess it up
You don't get to sing no mo
This is a high stakes situation

This space is
Lil Johnny graduating from pre-school
Henry got a new job
Josetta having a baby
Lem Jr. got accepted to college
Tasha just turned old enough
for shotguns and birth control
Ray Ray just turned old enough
for peach fuzz
This is an intervention
and a revival
   You are a guest
Consider your plate
a visitor's pamphlet
Big Mama's recliner is an altar
   When the call is made
You make sure to kneel there
and confess your appreciation,
give yourself to her grace,
and hope for an invitation
to return

Market Value

Jeremiah 29:11—For I know the plans I have for you," declares the Lord, "plans to prosper you and not to harm you, plans to give you hope and a future.

12-hour days,
extra shifts, and change jars
are an investment
A plan intended to be saving grace
Not for retirement
but for the 18 you will one day become
This portfolio is full of sweat, tears,
prayers, and luck
What is anticipated is maturity
and promising returns

There are projections
and expectations
Each shared moment
properly valuated according
to how it spurns growth
Food on table
Homework reviewed
Discipline in place
Pictures taken
Cheers given
Parties planned
Mistake made
Phone call to all
immediate family members
Achievement reached
Phone call to all
Immediate family members
Lessons learned
The easy way, the hard way

These options are intended
to show the world
that you are of good stock

Late nights and Sundays
are spent asking God
for there to be no crash,
no downturn
Only the continued rise of potential
Insider trading is not illegal here
It is a village raising a child
with as few losses as possible
Report cards and report backs
are market driven
That good book is a trade publication
full of stock tips
Speculation is best done
over a hot meal
and a stiff drink

Sanctimonious Service

Matt 11:28—"Come to me, all you who are weary and burdened, and I will give you rest."

I wonder if pious patriarchs,
those who see power and indulgence
as reward from up on high,
consider it an act of faith
when they lay down their burdens.
You know,
those they have consistently
marginalized and oppressed?

A Bug's Life

2 Pet 1:4—Through these he has given us his very great and precious promises, so that through them you may participate in the divine nature and escape the corruption in the world caused by evil desires.

There is a blessing come sunrise
when black cicadas
too often considered roaches
open their eyes
Able to breathe
Able to rise
Able to face another day
knowing they survived
the steel toed white supremacy
that came at nightfall

They Wood Hate Us Still

1 Pet 2:24—He himself bore our sins in his body on the tree, so that we might die to sins and live for righteousness: by his woulds you have been healed.

Growing up,
my favorite thing to do
was climb the tree in the yard
My mother would look
out the window in fear
Worry her son would fall
Worried her son would break
Me,
I climbed those limbs
with no thought of danger
Felt free
Felt strong

When they talk of hatred,
their favorite thing to show
is that picture of Marion, Indiana
We look
at that evening entertainment
Become saddened at a mother's loss
How the crowd wanted them broken
They hung
them boys from limbs
with no thought of repercussion
Felt justified
Felt strong

I look at that picture like stained glass
in the back of a sanctuary
where parishioners gather
to affirm their destiny manifest

A reminder of our ancestor's sacrifice
A reminder that some consider us unworthy
of any part of this empire
I'm aghast at the Pontius Pilate of it all
Even more appalled at the dedication
How they have made this madness institution
Indulged in a Babylon of feigned supremacy
Placed our broken past all around us
and told us to pray for better days

I know now
what that feeling was
that rose up in my mother
Made her scared to see
me in that tree
Worried it might be foreshadowing
Wondering if it might feel familiar
Fearful
they might
find me limp
with no pulse, punished
for feeling free
for feeling strong

Black Cloud

Mathew 9:13—But go and learn what this means: 'I desire mercy, not sacrifice.'For I have not come to call the righteous, but sinners."

When we hear thunder
Don't it sound like
Gabriel still trying to teach
God how to use that MPC
Like angels laughing when
he say that next album gone be fire
Cuz we been waiting on that reveal
with biblical anticipation
longer than we waited for Detox

When we hear gunshots
Don't it sound like
Job adlibbing over a Marvin Gaye
sample looped with the 808
of Lauren London's broken heart
Like Lucifer laughing at
a life of opulence turned tragedy
Cuz we been waiting on the proof
that a contract hit can be more billboard
than casket with as much delusion
as believing prosperity can be gospel

When the shells hit the ground
When that rumble crosses the sky
Don't it sound like a morse coded wonder
of am I still relevant?
Like sacrifice is too often
on earth as it is in heaven?
I mean, is anybody still listening?
I mean when them skies open
do we dance like ain't no other freedom?

I mean, when that beat drops
do we become overwrought with anxiety?
Is it all marveled at but never understood?
Confused by but never interrogated?
Mad at but never reconciled?
Does it sound like you ain't never
gone not remember me?
Does it hurt like why does it
got to be this way?
Then breaks you down like
I bet you didn't even see it coming

Emergency Room Trauma

Mark 16:17-18 17—And these signs will accompany those who
believe: In my name they will drive out demons; they will speak in
new tongues; 18 they will pick up snakes with their hands; and when
they drink deadly poison, it will not hurt them at all; they will place
their hands on sick people, and they will get well.

There is a college
that held the only Black
hospital from DC
to Georgia
A melanin miracle
where faith, dedication, and
aptitude in healing
patchworked crows whole

There is a college
that has held the children
of Black prayers
fed hope from Big Mama's Sunday
to graduation cookout
A historical melanin sanctuary
where education, nurturing, and
empowerment
would happen

It has found itself searching
for answers to how
it can best heal
the fragmentation of our futures
The building the hospital sat in
is an empty shell
that keeps alumni asking
when it will all once again
be made whole

Convenient Dismissal

Proverbs 18:13—"To answer before listening—that is folly and shame."

We wear clothes, shoes
Eat food
Buy furniture
All functional
All we have
All we can afford at the moment
We appreciate it
Treat it valuable

When we get the opportunity
Gain more resources
We change what we buy
Buy better
Buy longer lasting
Buy better made
Try new things
we wouldn't dare
risk before
Call it growth

When we are boys
We are taught how we should be
Shown the man we should become
by those who call themselves grown
Influenced by a culture that shapes us narrow
It's all we know
All we can be at that moment
We accept it
Treat it normal

When we find ourselves challenged to grow

Hear about the toxicity
of what we never had to be
Hear of the damage done
See the trauma caused
We should shift our thinking
Find new ways to live, to love
Look for healing from all
we were forced to be

We should make ourselves new
Know more
Be better
Seek to make it long lasting
Call it necessary

What a fragile thing it is
This masculine we are taught
to hold so tightly
If we stopped explaining it,
justifying it,
making excuses for it
Just listened
We would see
that it was never well made
Never healthy for us
Never sturdy enough
to support the weight of
the lives we want to live full
We would know
we needed to upgrade
and we would welcome
the opportunity to change

The King and James

2 Samuel 14:13—She replied, "Why don't you do as much for all the people of God as you have promised to do for me? You have convicted yourself in making this decision, because you have refuse to bring home your own banished son."

Tammy saw pastor at the corner store
Asked him how his day was going
Blessed he said
Asked him what he had planned for Sunday
A good word he said
Asked him how James was doing
Silence

See pastor hadn't had a good word
to say about the blessing God gave him
since James came out
So now silence is the only response
Head lowered in shame
like he praying

When his head lifts
Eyes watered
It's like God is trying to Noah
the ignorance out of him
and let him know that after the storm
is a rainbow

Sanctity and a Biscuit

Matthew 6:34—Therefore do not worry about tomorrow, for tomorrow will worry about itself. Each day has enough trouble of its own.

There is a reverie of wisdom
sitting in the dining room
of a Bojangles.
Elders, mostly men,
who have seen what a day's
hard work can build.
Homes, families, bonds, and
retirement.
They don't gather for the chicken,
they gather for the company.
This is a depot for truckers
who have made the long haul
and want a moment
to shoot the shit and tell stories.
Some are there every day.
Others come and go.
Anyone who is from the neighborhood
speaks as they enter and leave.
There is respect for that corner.
There is life in that corner.
Lived, struggled through, and
survived.

I sit in earshot each time I eat there.
My aim is to gather wisdom
and gossip.
To hear them place current events
in context both historical
and colored.
It is a class I get to partake in

for only the price of a combo.
A chance to see the future.
To learn possible.

I imagine the location
me and my brothers will choose.
Hope it will be filled with
the laughter and joy I see here.
The calm that comes with knowing
the worst is behind you
and any new day on two feet
is a blessing.
Gospel can be a greasy gathering.
I've seen the damage watering holes do.
Know it be a lot worse.
A worse I want to be
no sequel to.
If it not be café balcony,
beachfront villa, or
boat wading on water,
let it be this.
Dear God, let it be this.
Give me, us, us all
a corner of the
dining room.

Denial of God's Image

John 10:31-33 - 31—The Jews picked up stones again to stone Him. 32 Jesus answered them, "I showed you many good works from the Father; for which of them are you stoning Me?" 33 The Jews answered Him, "For a good work we do not stone You, but for blasphemy; and because You, being a man, make Yourself out to be God."

I have never understood
the hardened resolve
of those who enter into
a life with intent
to damage

That was until I met poets
who call it an adventure

Then set pencil to page
to verse an excuse,
as if applause is
exorcism for the demon
they brought into
another's home

If the victim survives
there will be no apology

Just delight at the idea
that stick and stones
are known demolition tools
but words can be
a painful lesson
in the denial of accountability

Bookshelves and God Complexes

Rom 12:2—Do not conform any longer to the pattern of this world but be transformed by the renewing of your mind. Then you will be able to test and approve what God's will is—his good, pleasing and perfect will.

They have turned bookshelves
into cults of personality
Secret handshakes, pledged allegiance,
ritualistic compromise, and
a gatekept password

Claimed that real estate
gated community
Membership only
Set the standard sacrifice
necessary to be seen
as accepted

They have turned bookshelves
into a bastion of bourgeois disillusionment
Named its overseers
a literary boule
Named its accolades right of passage
Not acknowledgement of
the breath and sweat put into
crafting a necessary mattering

They cannot do the same
with a community's hands
They cannot do the same
with a community's ears
Not their hearts
Not their souls
There are no confines

to the possible of that
blessed assurance

They demand a humbling
resembling a 40 year wait
A wilderness they say
will teach you to appreciate
the promise land
Call your pen to page
staff to a rock
If the water that flows
is credited to anything other
than the power they weld
then your atonement
is a snide dismissal

But they cannot rewrite
the people's faith in your words
They cannot deny the impact
They cannot dismiss the many you feed
with a feast prepared
with no more than pen and paper
Cannot call it no less than a miracle
For to witness is to believe,
is to know a great thing

So, write we will
And what a good and pleasing
will it is

Epilogue

This place here where poetry be
We call this a Sunday in Paradise
A meal fit for fellowship
This is a gathering of God's children
An escape from the burden
A refuge from the pain
A sanctuary, a haven for the hapless
who daydream with the sun
and find peace in the midst of the night
A beloved faithful who pray at midnight,
thank the Lord for another sunrise,
and don't falter at the sight of storm clouds
'Cause round here, when the sky sheds tears
we dance in the rain

This here be a Dirt Church
A body of believers
who laugh like mass choir,
pass wisdom like scripture,
and say amen in thanks
for the blessing of a good word
Walking down to that front porch
is like communion service
This slice of life
is my experiences, broken for you
Take it
So as you face your trials and tribulations,
you will remember that you
can overcome anything this world does to you
This ink is my covenant
poured out for the many
who don't get to speak for themselves
Drink it in
Let it be a sign that you do not

have to live in silence
Your voice is a revelation
we have been waiting for

WE CALL THIS a Sunday in Paradise
An invitation sent and received
A moment etched into time
A place in our souls
A chance to be inspired,
uplifted, encouraged, understood
An opportunity to learn,
express, connect, be recognized
You gone get full round here
You gone get fed round here
You gone get high, get drunk
You gone get loved round here
There is an abundance of it
We knew you were coming
Slaved in the kitchen to prepare this
Made everything just right
Dinner served here is a prayer circle,
a renewal of the spirit,
where you can rededicate yourself
to the mirror image of glory you are
Round here we pour a little something
straight no chaser
for those who like it to burn a bit
You know, Ignite a fire inside

Can't we be honest here?
Can't we share our hopes, fears,
dreams, and struggles here?
Ain't each story told a blessing or
a necessary evil?
Ain't it sometimes both?
Ain't each poem spoke a testimony?

Ain't it often right place and right on time?

This here Sunday in Paradise
is the opening of a home
for the purpose of
providing a place
to call welcome,
call inviting,
call accepting
call ours

Ain't no goodbye
Just a later laden understanding
that y'all gone come on back
round here again
Because ain't no
celebration like this
Ain't no freedom like this
Ain't no glory, ain't no amen like this
Ain't no better knowing
Ain't no better feeling
Ain't no better way
to BE YOU
right now
than to BE
right HERE

About the Poet

Dasan Ahanu is an award-winning poet and performance artist, public speaker, community organizer, educator, scholar and emcee born and raised in Raleigh, North Carolina. He is an Alumni Nasir Jones Fellow at Harvard's Hip Hop Archive and Research Institute, resident artist at the St. Joseph's Historic Foundation/Hayti Heritage Center, and visiting lecturer at the University of North Carolina-Chapel Hill. He has performed across the country, appeared on national radio and TV, published three books of poetry, been featured in various periodicals and released numerous recordings. He works with organizations and institutions to develop effective arts strategies to enhance their work in the community. Dasan is currently managing a grant funded initiative as the Rothwell Mellon Program Director for Creative Futures with Carolina Performing Arts. He swings a mean pen and represents the SOUTH.

Milton Keynes UK
Ingram Content Group UK Ltd.
UKHW010623080324
438959UK00001B/88